Thomas Alva Edison

By Wil Mara

Consultant
Nanci R. Vargus, Ed.D.
Assistant Professor of Literacy
University of Indianapolis, Indianapolis, Indiana

Children's Press®
A Division of Scholastic Inc.
New York   Toronto   London   Auckland   Sydney
Mexico City   New Delhi   Hong Kong
Danbury, Connecticut

Designer: Herman Adler Design
Photo Researcher: Caroline Anderson
The photo on the cover shows Thomas Edison.

Library of Congress Cataloging-in-Publication Data

Mara, Wil.
  Thomas Alva Edison / by Wil Mara.
      p. cm. – (Rookie biographies)
Summary: An introduction to the life of Thomas Alva Edison, whose many inventions included the phonograph and the light bulb.
Includes bibliographical references and index.
  ISBN 0-516-21843-3 (lib. bdg.)   0-516-25822-2 (pbk.)
  1. Edison, Thomas A. (Thomas Alva), 1847-1931–Juvenile literature.
2. Inventors–United States–Biography–Juvenile literature. 3. Electric engineers–United States–Biography–Juvenile literature. [1. Edison, Thomas A. (Thomas Alva), 1847-1931. 2. Inventors. 3. Scientists.]
I. Title. II. Series: Rookie biography
  TK140.E3M26 2003
  621.3'092–dc22

                                    2003013673

9 10 11 12 13 R 13 12   62

What do you think these young scientists are doing?

4

Maybe they are inventing something, like these scientists.

Where do ideas for new things come from? They come from inventors.

Thomas Alva Edison was one of the world's greatest inventors.

8

Edison was born on February 11, 1847, in Milan, Ohio. He was the youngest child in his family.

Edison did not go to school for very long. His mother taught him at home.

Edison always asked lots of questions. He did experiments to find the answers.

Sometimes they were messy, like his egg experiment.

One day, Edison saw a goose sitting on an egg. Someone said the goose was trying to hatch the egg.

Edison tried to hatch an egg, too. He sat on the egg and broke it!

Edison built his first lab when he was ten years old. He did many experiments there.

The smells were so horrible that Edison's mother made him get a job instead.

He sold newspapers and candy on trains.

16

One day, Edison saved the son of a railroad station master. The boy was almost run over by a train.

To thank Edison, the station master taught him how to use a telegraph. A telegraph uses electricity to send messages through wires.

Edison made a better telegraph.

Then in 1876, he built a lab in Menlo Park, New Jersey. That is where Edison invented the phonograph. It played music.

Next, Edison and his helpers
tried to make the light bulb.

However, light bulbs need electricity to work.

Most people did not have electricity. So Edison helped build the first power plant.

Edison invented more than 1,000 things. His inventions made him famous.

People called him the "Wizard of Menlo Park."

Edison also invented a box that showed movies. People watched the movies through a hole on top of the box.

Edison never stopped trying new things. He died on October 18, 1931. He was 84.

An early movie theater

Words You Know

inventor

phonograph

power plant

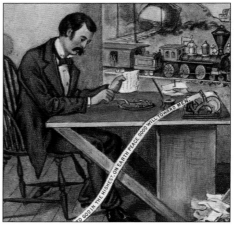

scientists

telegraph

Index

About the Author

More than fifty published books, including biographies, bear Wil Mara's name. He has written both fiction and nonfiction, for both children and adults. He lives with his family in northern New Jersey.

Photo Credits